The Insider's Guide to Grief

Stacy S. Remke

© Stacy S. Remke 2013

ISBN: 978-0-9899198-2-1

Cover Image:
old tree photo©istockphoto.com/mammuth

Interior Images:
Spring Colorful Foggy Forest - Sun Beams©istockphoto.com/konradlew
amazing beech tree 2©istockphoto.com/graafisk

"The wound is the place where the light enters you..."

—Rumi

For Sara, Andy and Sandy,
who were my close companions in grief

Table of Contents

Introduction

This guide is intended to help shed a little light on the path of grief that you face when someone you love dies. My hope is that it may be helpful as you embark upon the journey through grief yourself, or perhaps try to understand what someone else is going through. It is intended to be a kind of "user's guide," for those who grieve. This is not an academic treatise or a research study, but it is informed by my own experiences of loss, being a friend to others in their grief, as well as my fifty-some years as person who has walked with many others through loss experiences of all kinds.

It is organized in short sections. Please feel free to dip in where ever it is helpful, or when you feel the need. Put it down when you need a break.

I hope this is helpful.

Most of all, I wish you peace in your heart.

The Arc of Grief

While everyone's experience with grief is uniquely theirs, there do seem to be some common rhythms or patterns to it for most people. To me, it seems like a sort of arc, or bell curve, with lighter feeling episodes on either end—coming into it, and going out of it—with perhaps a few bumps or hiccups personally determined along the way. It may help to know a little bit about what to expect.

In my travels, I have met many people who have survived the death of a loved one, walked through the rituals, the funeral, the tasks of laying to rest, and felt very relieved. They are relieved they have gotten through the awful moment of loss, they are exhausted by the process, and they have perhaps been buoyed by the help and support of others. After those first few weeks, they might say things like, "this isn't so bad…" and "I'll be OK…" And that is a good attitude.

The good news is: you will be OK.

The bad news is: this is only the beginning.

Grief is a long and uneven road to healing. There are more intense and less intense periods, and people seem to have differences when it comes to what is hardest or most manageable for them. So with some reasonable room for variations and special circumstances, you can probably expect it to go something like this:

First, the loss

When someone you care about, and organize your days around, and count on dies, it is like a tearing apart of the world—your world. The pain of loss is great, and feels shattering. Whether you anticipated the death, or were surprised by it doesn't really matter. No matter what preparation you can do—and I'm sure whatever one can do to prepare does help—there is just really no way to prepare for or avoid the intense shock and pain of loss.

The emotional pain of loss can be likened to a wave: crashing, and then ebbing. If you can think of it like a series of waves, then focusing on balance, and learning to surf those waves, or at least hold your footing as they flow around you, can be a very helpful strategy. When they come crashing, those waves can threaten to knock us over.

Try to stay in the present moment, breathe in and out slowly, and remind yourself of the constancy of the earth, floor, the chair there to support you, the roof and the sky there to shelter you.

There are also waves of disbelief and perhaps waves of relief, of anger, sadness or love, depending upon the situation, and what has happened for you. And here's the thing about feelings: resistance is futile. The more you resist them, the greater they seem to grow. Try to let them have their moment. They are feelings: they ebb and flow.

The immediate future

In the first weeks after the death, things can be quite busy and full. Friends and relatives rally around; food is brought; funerals are planned and rituals held. All the good intentions of others can be supportive, and also distracting. And if the loss is colored by difficult relationships between survivors and the person who died, then lots of energy can get used up managing the complicated interactions that can occur as families reconnect and interact under stress.

Eventually, people go away again, and perhaps you sleep. A lot. Or not at all. Both these reactions can be considered normal.

Different styles maybe. You return to work, or school, or those normal routines that keep life going and can only bear so much neglect. As these tasks demand attention and begin to re-assert themselves, it might feel like a bit of relief to get back to something familiar, and to think on things beyond yourself.

If we think of grief as being something like a roller coaster, this is perhaps the first little dip. I remember thinking things like: "well, I'm ok, so why not…" and "there's no good reason not to…" when friends asked me over, or I couldn't quite put my finger on why I didn't want to do stuff. Then the sad feelings, or the tears, or the fatigue would hit me. Or I caught a cold. Or something else seemed to get in the way of feeling back to normal. It was "always something." And basically, it was all grief.

Next, grief settles in to stay a while

So the first few months are pretty sad, teary, heavy and tiring. You get kind of used to it, and gradually learn to manage within this new reality. The loss of your person creates a kind of hole in the fabric of your world, and it takes a while to just get in the rhythm of putting one foot in front of another. This new world may seem harsh, too loud and bright and fast. Or, it might seem muted, gray, devoid of color or music. After a couple months of this, you can start to feel like this will go on forever. You may find you have memories of your person—sweet ones, or upsetting ones—just pop into your head, often at the most surprising times. These can be distressing just in how unexpected they can be, and how much emotion they can carry with them.

> I remember after my dad died, I used to see him in my mind's eye in several characteristic poses—leaning on his golf club at the 18th hole, sitting in his familiar chair and smiling at me, and also as he was just before he died: much too thin, ashen, and with an anxious look in his eye as he managed sharp intakes of breath, as if he tried

> *to suck in bursts of pain. The awful images were much*
> *more frequent at first, sometimes distracting me from*
> *what I was trying to do, but they did subside, leaving*
> *room for more pleasing memories that comforted rather*
> *than saddened me.*

Don't be surprised if just when you might feel you are getting back on your feet—2 or 3 months in—you find you hit a new wall. Fatigue, sadness that can't be ignored anymore because of the fatigue, and irritability because of all the fatigue and sadness tend to well up and threaten to take over. I think this comes from the cumulative effects of coping with the waves of grief, all the necessary adjustments, and also keeping life moving along. You can imagine the storehouses of energy have been used up by subtle and obvious processes. The gas tank is empty. I remember there were times I felt quite beat up inside, but it didn't show to anyone else. I was in a brittle state, ready to snap at the least amount of provocation. People talked to me like I was my usual self, not noticing how checked out I was, how preoccupied and self-involved I was.

The long road

The months between roughly three and ten after their loss tend to be the most arduous for many people. The reserves of energy are used up, and it seems harder to get them replenished. Things that used to refresh the body and spirit may not seem to do the trick anymore, and maybe there aren't energies to go exploring new directions. Then again, there are those whose grief takes them in the direction of activity. They try new groups and hobbies, throw themselves into new routines, or organize everything. This works for them too.

It's all about noticing what's happening for you, and letting it be that way.

The demands on the bereaved person's body, mind and spirit are high. The process of grieving demands conscious as well as unconscious attention. The laundry still needs doing, the kids need attention, and the grocery shopping still needs to get done. It's a rough patch. There's no getting around it. You may look like your usual self on the outside, so people may expect you to act like the you they know. It may be hard to crank it up, and they may forget or not notice the burden of grief you still carry.

This stage also reflects a process that is taking place underground. Not unlike the tulip bulbs gathering strength beneath the surface of the earth, waiting until the weather is right for blooming. It seems to require quite a bit of energy, though you may not see where it is going, or what the results are right away. It seems at this stage that our psyche is helping us to re-knit the world back together, after that important thread that was our relationship with our beloved has been severed and our world has come unraveled.

> *I would come home from work and take a little nap before dinner, walk the dog, eat something, watch a little TV and go to bed. That was all I seemed able to do for weeks and weeks. I bored myself. I was working on a committee project that I was trying hard to keep up with, not only because I had made a commitment, but it was something that helped me focus on something bigger than my own problems. One night, the project director called me to discuss some issue or another. After I hung up, I felt relieved I had been able to be focused and coherent enough. A couple minutes later, the phone rang. It was the project director again. "I just wanted you to know that when we were talking, I really heard the grief in your voice." I felt the tears well up, and while I choked back a sob making its way up, I thanked him for noticing. It was good to be perceived in my true state. It was a relief to cry, too, and to be able to feel more than just tired.*

So if you are finding it hard to put one foot in front of another, or to keep up with work, kids and laundry, know that you are expending tremendous energy underground, reshaping the world from the inside out. The days for reaching and blooming are still ahead. Some people will notice and be patient. Others will wonder why you haven't gotten "over it" yet. Know that you are moving through on multiple levels at once, in the ways that make sense for your own self.

Light peeks in

As time goes on, you get somewhat used to living with the burdens of grief. You come to recognize the loss is real, that your beloved is not coming back, and that this is the new world.

Gradually, some energy returns, and the ability to focus and accomplish things improves a bit. Maybe you feel like you can breathe and sleep again. Maybe you feel like you can gather the steam to go out and do things, see friends, and return to the things that brought you joy before. At least for some moments, you start to catch glimpses of feeling better.

This can be a tricky part. For some of us, it can feel hard to recover. It may feel like moving further away from our beloved, or somehow beginning to let them go feels like a whole other loss. It helped me to remember that my beloved would not want me to live my life only focused on the loss. It also helped me to remember that I didn't forget them. I could call up memories, or talk to friends and relatives to relive stories and remember.

But letting go is another layer of loss. When grief has become a certain kind of constant friend, a new normal, and a comfort in some ways, it can be hard to emerge from it. Our grief can be distracting us from the hard work of re-knitting the world back together, too.

Observe your own process. Allow whatever is happening to be true for you, for now. Some people find the first weeks and months are the worst, and then the hardest part gradually lessens over time. Others find they have peaks and valleys of intensity over the course of a year or two. Still others may find that there is an early and constant intensity, and a certain companion quality of grief that never quite leaves them, even as they adjust to life after loss. All these patterns of adjustment can be considered normal.

The anniversary season

As the anniversary time of the loss rolls around, many people seem to experience a resurgence of grief again. It may be in the form of bouts of sadness, or fatigue, or renewed awareness of the magnitude of the loss. Physical signs and symptoms may re-emerge for a time. This may go one for weeks or even a couple months. Then, once the anniversary has passed, the dust seems to settle again. With a deep sigh and rolling of shoulders, notice how far you have come. You have survived the worst of it. It may help to notice that you have *already* survived.

I think there is something to getting through a whole year, a complete turn of the earth, that is healing. The slant of light, the state of fecundity or desolation of the natural world in seasons, reminds us at some deep level of the turnings of the grieving season too.

Signs and Symptoms
of Grief

     I have noticed that in our culture we don't talk about the many, varied signs and symptoms of grief that many people encounter. The fact is that grief affects all the dimensions of our being. We have signals from body, mind and spirit that reflect the depth of the process, and the deep layers of reorganization required to get through it. When we don't know these signs and symptoms reflect normal grieving, it is easy to worry about ourselves. We may wonder if we are seriously ill or going crazy, losing ourselves in the whole process. This has the effect of making grieving worse: the burdens are enough without adding additional anxiety. So let's talk about some of those common experiences here.

Body
     Our physical self is of course closely intertwined with our emotional, spiritual and thinking, perceiving selves. Our bodies talk to us in the language they know: body twinges, aches, symptoms and processes. These signals are our body's way of telling us that changes

are happening, and energies are being channeled to and absorbed by the process.

Grieving people commonly experience a whole host of physical indicators of the grief process. I've noticed they don't often mention this part. These can include headaches, stomach aches, nausea, more frequent colds and flu because the immune system is stressed by grief, a pit in the stomach, or hollow feelings in the abdomen, joint pains and generalized achiness, fatigue, sleep disruptions, feelings of the heart racing or palpitations, tingling sensations, hunger, loss of appetite, lust or sexual urgency, and weight gain and/or loss.

These are just some of the variety of things someone can experience when they are grieving. I think the best way to think of it is that your body, as part of your whole self, is undergoing major adjustments too. As your body supports these adaptations, energy is needed and is drawn in for the project. As a result it is not available for some of the other things we used to take for granted, like work and family and raking the yard.

> *Right after my dad died, about 3 or 4 weeks in, I felt the loss in my body. I felt vaguely nauseous all the time. This lasted for about three months. I lost weight. I was a little satisfied about that. Then, the nausea subsided, and I felt a pit in my stomach. I felt hollowness. I ate more. And then some more. Even so, the pit didn't go away for a long time. I gained the weight back. Oh well.*

> *Around the time each of my parents died I found myself single again (long story, and yes: I did take it to therapy…) and also experiencing a lot of lusty impulses. There were a couple occasions I may not have made the best choices about how to scratch this itch. It felt like an urgent matter sometimes to indulge desires. Then they would collapse almost as fast as they came, almost like running out of gas. I came to think of these impulses as*

reminders that in spite of my grief, my job now was to be alive. These impulses of the life force were strong and compelling. They were also frustrating and confusing. Such is grief.

Guilt

Some people really struggle with feelings of guilt after the death of a loved one. This can take many forms. Often, it is related to a sense of missed chances: *why didn't I do this or that? I should have said it..., or why didn't I ...If only..."*

For others, it may be about a specific action right before the death. Maybe they gave the last dose of pain medicine, or the last bath, and they worry that caused the person's death. There is always one last thing when someone dies: the last meeting, the last phone call, the last meal or dose of medicine. There is always a last thing in each life. Yet that is rarely what actually caused their death. It was the disease, or the accident, or perhaps their great age.

Guilt presumes we have control. In so many instances, we are caught in the grips of forces so much greater than our own. We make choices every day, based on what we know and hope for. Such are the daily dilemmas of human life.

If you can, be gentle with yourself, know you did the best you could at the time, and humbly seek forgiveness from yourself, from others, from the beloved dead, for all those moments we failed to be our very best selves.

Mind

There are tricks of the mind in grief for sure. They are at times comforting and reassuring and at other times distressing. No, you are not losing your mind: you are grieving. People will often describe feeling "foggy" in their brain, having trouble remembering things: names, phone numbers, your own way home... It can be upsetting when it happens.

Not only have you lost your loved one, now you're losing your marbles too?

No, it is temporary.

If you think of this as another sign of all the hard work going on underground, it makes sense. The energy for clear thinking and recall has been disrupted, just like everything else. The circuits are down. People describe feeling confusion, an inability to think clearly, "foggy," numb, and "blank." This phenomenon can occur at the most inopportune times. And let's face it, it can be frightening.

Pause, breathe, and try to refocus.

There is another kind of mind experience that can happen too. Sometimes grieving people describe hearing voices, or catching a glimpse of their loved one. This is mysterious, but quite normal. Again: you're not crazy, you're grieving.

> *There was a period where I could hear my mom's voice, sounding just like the last message she left on my answering machine: "Are you there? Are you there? Call me back sometime..." I came to think of it as a gesture of her spirit, calling to me, and reminding me of the sound of her voice. The experience faded over time, and I sometimes miss being able to recall the exact sound of her voice.*

> *There were other times I could hear her voice calling out my name, sometimes urgently, like when I was in trouble when I was a kid or when she wanted us to come RIGHT NOW. You know how moms can sound.*

Spirit

Being bereaved seems to present some natural opportunities to experience spiritual insights. These may range from mysterious experiences of feeling a presence, or rich awareness of the teachings of faith, a quest for connecting with the spirit of the departed through mediums or hoping for ghosts. It seems a common thing for grievers to seek some kind of explanation, or find some meaning behind the experience of loss. This is a very personal thing, informed by such things as personality, beliefs, and experiences in grief. Some may find that the beliefs they had before their loss are strengthened and affirmed by their perceptions in grief. Others may find them challenged and questioned by the reality of their pain. For some, spiritual experiences go hand in hand with religious faith. For others, these may diverge. For still others their experience of spirit has nothing to do with religious practices.

I would suggest that the part that matters most is how you feel your spirit is engaged with something larger. My friend once said that you can find clues to your spiritual resources. When you feel overwhelmed or completely at sea, notice what it is that starts to come in to the picture that lifts you up again. The beauty found in nature? Simple times spent with your family? A funny movie that makes you laugh? Finding a moment of peace to relax into? Look for even small hints of ease or renewal. These will show the way.

You may also find that you notice things differently. There may be a tender beauty in a child's trusting smile, or an overwhelming sense of connection with All That Is as you gaze at the moon on a crisp winter evening. You have found a new lens through which to view your experience and especially, your loss.

The Buddhists talk about how when your heart breaks, it is breaking open: getting bigger, and stronger.

> *About a year or so after my dad died, I had an experience*
> *where right in the middle of some elaborate dream of*
> *driving up a hillside with a friend, a strong and vital*
> *image of my dad popped in, standing in a very familiar*
> *way, and speaking to me directly. I said to him in my*
> *dream that I was sorry for ways that I had disappointed*
> *him. He looked at me very directly and said that no, he*
> *was sorry, and that he understood so much more now,*

and wanted to say how proud he was of me. This dream had a very soothing and healing effect on me. When I was sharing it with my counselor later, she surprised me by asking me: was it a dream, or a visit? At that moment I suddenly knew it had been a visit.

The Artifacts of Someone Else's Life

One of the weirder aspects of grief is the fact that things outlive their people. As we come to terms with the loss of our beloved, we still see the artifacts of their life all around us. There are their clothes, their books, their furniture and knick-knacks, leftovers in the fridge. The scraps of handwriting, and the unfinished projects awaiting completion on the kitchen counter: life interrupted midstream.

These things seem to almost reverberate with the absence of our loved one, accentuating the empty place that was created by their death. And these things need attention. Apartments need to be emptied out. The parceling out of belongings needs to occur. The last talismans of their life need to be treasured. And the junk needs to be disposed of. Sometimes it can be difficult to tell the difference between the two.

When my mom died we needed to pack up her apartment
and do something with all her stuff in about 3 weeks.
We basically threw it all into boxes and put it into

my basement. There was a very rainy spring, and the basement leaked. Lots of the stuff got wet, and some was damaged. When we got into sorting and throwing stuff away, it was tempting to see everything as a treasure, a precious relic of mom's life. I picked up a notebook of pen scratchings and notes from some lecture or talk she had been to. It was moldy and waterlogged, but also held her own handwriting, familiar and comforting. I held it up, and said "Look, it's..." and my sister-in-law said "...trash," as she took it from my hand. And of course she was right. It went into the dumpster. I did save some other small notebooks with her writing in them, not water -logged, not moldy, and easy to store. Not everything perhaps, but enough.

The point is, it is important to take the time you need to sort through and make choices about what is left behind. Maybe there is a will or some record of who gets what, which can help. There is time to make decisions about these things. Attend to the task in the way that makes the most sense for you and your family. Know too that these things are not your person. They remind and evoke memories, but they are just things. Choose those things that are most meaningful for you. Curate a selection of artifacts that bring you comfort. It may take a while to figure out what to keep. That's OK.

People

We all rely on others to help us through hard times. It is a part of being human. When you are grieving, often there are people close to you that are also grieving. That can be a comfort: you are not in this alone. Then again, it can be hard when you are grieving out of sync with one another. When your spouse needs to get busy and try and distract themselves on the same day you really need to talk and share, it is a trial. When the kids need to be managed and all you want to do is crawl back to bed, it can feel like an enormous burden. Friends that go back to their own lives, as you would expect them to, may not notice that you are still in the very normal yet deep phases of grief and cannot quite be there in the way they are used to. Then there are the ones who emerge as steadfast and patient, allowing you your own process, and willing to listen to the umpteenth story you need to tell. There is nothing like grief to really find out who your friends are.

If you can, be aware enough to let others know what you need, are asking for, or going through, that will help. Try and be specific. Acknowledge their patience and concern. And share: try to avoid burdening a few key people by drawing in some others. If your spouse can't be there for you today because of their own grief, can you call someone else? A wide circle of support can help spread the support around. This is a principle of physics actually: a broader base is better able to support the load.

If you find you need more support and it isn't there in your natural circle of friends and family, know that there are other resources out there. This might be an excellent time to engage a counselor, or to attend a support group. Being with others who understand, and sharing your stories can be healing.

If you are worried about how you are doing, or how you will get through, see if finding a helpful counselor can help you over the roughest patches. For most of us, it's less about needing therapy, and more about seeking reassurance, and a boost of energy from someone else who is not burdened by grief.

There are some people who do struggle more, and can't seem to see the way through their grief. It may be their loss was particularly traumatic, or their preparedness to cope was otherwise diminished at the time. For these folks, grief may take longer to process, and a therapist may be very important for helping to regain a foothold on the path, to see your way further down the road to healing.

Conclusion

If you can, honor your own process. Let it unfold like a difficult and fascinating story, informing and enlightening you as you go. Know that you are the expert about what you need at any given time, though it might take a little effort to figure out what that is. The clearer you can be about what is happening for you, and what you need, the better able you are to ask others to help you.

Sometimes I wonder if the nature of grief isn't a bit like child birth? We suffer great pain in the process of transformation, yet in her wisdom, nature offers us a veil after it is over. I remember that in my various griefs, I suffered, and wept, was sleepless, and cried out. But now, I can't really remember exactly what that pain was like: only that I had it. And I am grateful for that.

My mother had a poster in the kitchen: the picture was a photo of a beautiful, weather worn natural stone arch rising out of an expansive crystal blue sea.

"The only way out is through…" it said.

Know this:
Even as you are suffering, you are not broken.

Bless your heart.

Acknowledgements

I have been blessed with many wonderful family members and friends who helped me on my journeys through grief. While they are too numerous to mention each by name, a few need special mentions: Sara and Andy, of course; Leslie, Sandy R., Kate B., Doug and Gail, Jerry F., Ione H., Bean, and Krista W. who always seemed to show up at the right moments.

Thanks to my writing friends for all their help: to my Writing Group—Merodie, Ann, Sara and Hilary—for their support for this project all along the way, and their helpful comments. Thanks also to Krista W. for her wise feedback and insights on early drafts. Thanks to those who took time and energy in the midst of their own grief to read early drafts: Michelle R., LaDonna M., Melis A., Elinor A. I appreciate feedback from professional colleagues who read drafts and contributed insights as well: Donna E., and Jody C.

Thank you, Patti Frazee for helpful guidance and editorial assistance needed to get this work out into the wider world.

I learned a great deal from those in my professional life who allowed me to know them in their grief. To each of them that I am unable to name, thank you for your trust, and for your stories that helped me to understand better, and hopefully to help others a little better.

Notes

Notes

Notes

Notes

Made in United States
North Haven, CT
06 May 2022